Christ Triumphant

and other hymns by

Michael Saward

written between

1962 – 2006

Jubilate Hymns Ltd

First published in Great Britain in 2006
by Jubilate Hymns Ltd

ISBN 0-9505589-90

Printed in Great Britain by
CPD (Wales) Ltd, Ebbw Vale.

Penpress,
39 Chesham Road,
Brighton.
East Sussex
BN2 1NB

Jubilate Hymns Ltd
4, Thorne Park Road,
Chelston,
Torquay. Devon.
TQ2 6RX

For my colleagues and friends
in the Jubilate Group
to whom I owe so much
over so many years.

It might be helpful to know that the two
Michaels pronounce their surnames
'Born' and 'Sayw'd'.

Foreword
by *Michael Baughen, formerly Bishop of Chester*

When Archbishop Michael Ramsey had his 80th birthday he quipped 'my age has caught up with my face.' When Michael Saward (who was for some years Radio and TV officer for Michael Ramsey) became a Canon of St Paul's Cathedral his ministry role caught up with his talents and capabilities. Although he had distinguished himself in parochial ministry, in the media, in Synod, in church politics and as a preacher ('never, but never boring' said the *Church of England Newspaper)* he was now serving in a huge place of worship with its greatly influential ministry. St Paul's Cathedral was built to the glory of God and its magnificence expresses that; it is based on the shape of the cross, has great supporting pillars and a strong foundation; it enables everyone to worship as there is no separation by a choir screen; it is crowned with daring and flair by the glorious dome. All of that is expressed in Michael Saward, the hymn-writer. God is very much at the centre and he captures the scale with 'The earth is yours, O Lord' from Psalm 24. Yet he is concerned to speak of God in Trinity whenever suitable and to address hymns to the Holy Spirit as well as to the Father and the Son. His translation of the Orthodox 'O Trinity, O Trinity' is near to his heart and his hymn 'All-creating heavenly giver' is fully Trinitarian.

The foundations and pillars are strongly emphasised. Those who seem blind to the many assurances of salvation in Scripture and who would replace pillars by a swamp of doubting, were and are furious with his exhilarating 'These are the facts', which is absolutely four-square on Scripture. His most famous hymn by far is 'Christ triumphant', loved and used all round the world, and here not only are the basic foundations of who Christ is and what he came to do clearly expressed but they are lifted into worship in every verse. Another rightly popular hymn is 'Lord of the cross of shame', a very firm favourite with me, as it touches the heart and enables heart-worship of, and prayer to, one's Lord and Saviour.

Michael has seen gaps and has filled them, not least in hymns for weddings and baptisms, one of which, 'Baptised in water', is his second most-used hymn. Chester Cathedral choir chose to sing 'Christmas for God's holy people' when they came with me on a TV programme.

Michael loves to see church worship alive and real but not with endless flimsy 'I feel' songs. Luther said of his own hymns that they were more influential than his preaching! Michael knows the importance of theology lifted into worship. He has also been passionate to see hymnody in contemporary language.

The daring of Wren's dome at St Paul's is akin to Michael's character. He has always had a boldness (some friends say he is larger than life) and this appears from time to time in his hymnody. Only Michael could have written a hymn beginning 'Fire of God, titanic Spirit', which later, under pressure from those who objected to the link with pagan mythology, and the tragic fate of the ocean liner, became a new verse three ('Fire of God, volcanic Spirit'), following on two new stanzas, 'Wind of God, dynamic Spirit' and ' Voice of God, prophetic Spirit'. Thus the Spirit breathes, speaks, and burns and that word 'volcanic' (replacing 'titanic') retains the authentic Saward touch!

The skills of hymn-writing have developed in Michael to such an extent that he has become a foremost evaluator of hymns written by others (old and new). His eye quickly knows whether a hymn is poor or not; whether there are bad rhymes or metres; whether there are resonances or sounds that do not match or are repeated too much and so on. Some have been hurt by his remarks or perhaps they thought their work was perfect and sometimes claimed that the Holy Spirit gave it to them so it could not be wrong!); others have welcomed the evaluation, acted on it and have greatly improved. Michael's expertise is a gift to the church. In particular we see how this worked out in his outstanding chairmanship of the words committees for *Hymns for Today's Church* and *Sing Glory*, (the former taking ten years of thorough work).

Michael is a gourmet and in his splendid hymns he has given us good food to uplift our worship, enabling us to express it in relevant theology, with rich and refreshing words that stir the heart. What a contrast to some of the worship material around today! The whole church is in Michael's debt, and we can go on worshipping our glorious God with Michael's fine hymns for many years to come.

Michael Baughen

Contents

This book contains the texts of seventy five hymns and psalm para-phrases written, and in many cases published, between 1962 and 2006. The opening hymn, 'Christ Triumphant', has pride of place being by far the most popular of my hymns (though not, I confess, my own favourite).

After that, all the remainder are set out in alphabetical order. This is not in my judgment the best way to present a major hymn-book which is almost always a better product if it is arranged in either a thematic or a liturgical pattern. The alphabetical solution does, however, make more sense in an author's collection especially, if like this one, it is a brief selection.

I have actually written something over one hundred hymns but, as is the case with most hymn-writers, not all are worth publication and so I have selected some seventy-five to mark the beginning of my 75th year in May 2006.

As regards tunes, I have selected those which are my own pref-erence. No hymn-writer across the centuries has had the luxury of being able to decide exactly which tunes will be used in those hymn-books which contain his works. That may or may not have been to the benefit of the texts, the congregations, or the author's convictions. In a personal collection like this one, the author has the advantage of informing the world of his own wishes, which may merely exhibit his prejudices or even, occasionally, advise future editors of what to avoid if they are to ensure that words and music are to provide a happy and creative blend.

What is a Hymn ?

The following definition by Michael Saward was published in The Times newspaper in October 1995.

' A hymn is a series of connected verses, usually addressed in worship to one or all of the Persons of the Holy Trinity, logically developing a Christian theme, usually in metrical and rhyming form, to a tune capable of being sung by a congregation.'

Reproduction of Copyright

Permission to reproduce any of these texts (all of which are in copyright) may be obtained in the UK from Jubilate Hymns, 4, Thorne Park Road, Chelston. Torquay. TQ2 6RX or, in the USA, from Hope Publishing Co. 380, South Main Place, Carol Stream. Il 60188. Elsewhere please contact Jubilate.

In all reproduction, the correct copyright ascription must be added at the foot of the text, namely,
© Michael Saward/Jubilate Hymns

These texts are the definitive version (and earlier wording is no longer authorised for reproduction).

The author asks that the layout, punctuation, and capitalisation be followed wherever possible. This will assist both the sense and the singing.

Copyright of tunes, where printed out, is owned by the composer and/or arranger and details can be obtained from Jubilate Hymns at the above address.

Canon Michael Saward - a brief biography

Michael was born at Blackheath in South East London on 14th May 1932 He grew up in Petts Wood, was educated at Eltham College (overlapping briefly with his fellow hymn-writer Chris Idle) and became a practising Christian in 1946 at a Crusader Camp. After his National Service, most of which he spent as a subaltern in the Royal West African Frontier Force in Accra, Ghana – then the Gold Coast – he read Theology at Bristol and played cricket for the University for four years.

He was ordained Priest in Canterbury Cathedral by Archbishop Geoffrey Fisher in 1957 and served curacies in Croydon and Edgware – two London suburbs. From 1964-67 he was Secretary of Liverpool Council of Churches before spending five years as Radio and Television Officer to Archbishop Michael Ramsey. He then became Vicar of St Matthew's in Fulham (1972-78) and Ealing Parish Church (1978-91). At that time he was President of the House of Clergy of the Willesden Area Synod in London Diocese and a Prebendary of St Paul's Cathedral.

Among the large number of councils and committees on which he served, he was a member of the General Synod (1975-95), a Church Commissioner (1978-93), on the Church of England Evangelical Council (1976-93) and Chairman of the Billy Graham Media Task Group of London's Mission '89. Later, in 2000, he was a judge in The Times *Preacher of the Year* Competition.

Prior to his retirement, he was Canon Treasurer of St Paul's Cathedral (1991-2000). During that time he was made a Freeman of the City of London and also a member of the Athenaeum. Inevitably he met most of the Royal family and the Lord Mayors of London. On one memorable occasion he shook hands with fifty-five Heads of State from around the world at the Cathedral door! Sadly, it fell to him to announce the death of Princess Diana from the pulpit, and preach three times, within hours of her fatal accident

An author (14 books), a prize-winning journalist and hymn-writer, (over 100 hymns), a regular broadcaster (650 programmes), religious adviser to the film *Cromwell*, and holder of a Winston Churchill travelling fellowship, he has been Words Editor of three hymnbooks (*Hymns for Today's Church, Sing Glory*, and *Sing to the Lord*, (the St Paul's Cathedral supplementary book). He has been a Director and Chairman of Jubilate Hymns and a member of the Hymn Society (with six years on its committee).

He has preached and spoken in over three hundred and fifty churches and cathedrals in half a dozen countries including the USA (including Canterbury, Westminster Abbey, St Paul's, Liverpool, Norwich, Rochester, Londonderry, Guildford, Miami, and Westminster Roman Catholic cathedral). He has lectured on the QE2 and been trustee of a castle! For seven years he was a chaplain at a WW1 Somme mine crater and preached twice in the Tower of London. He has survived!

He met Jackie at University, married her in 1956 and they have four children, seven grandchildren and one great grandson. His interests include military history, classical music, opera, reading (2600 books to date), travel and cricket.

So why does he write hymns? Sometimes he is commissioned to do so. Sometimes in order to enter competitions (he has been a winner of two national ones). Sometimes because 'the urge to put pen to paper remains powerful'. Lastly, and most important of all, because, he says, 'crafting words to the glory of God, the Holy Trinity, to be used in Christian worship, is one of the most deeply satisfying ways of joining heart, mind, and hand in adoration of Jesus, my Lord and Saviour'.

Preface

What, we might ask, is the purpose of a hymn ? The *Report of the Archbishops' Commission on Church Music* (1992) gives us a useful answer. 'Hymns', it tells us, 'provide a rich resource for personal devotion' and, it adds, 'they articulate personal spiritual experience. They reveal the inner weather of the human heart'. So far, so good.

Such a definition, however, fails to explain what a hymn is. Rather, it tells us what a hymn does and puts all the emphasis on the subjective response of the singer.

One of the very earliest descriptions of Christian hymn-singing comes from the famous words of Pliny the Younger. He tells the Roman Emperor Trajan, early in the second century, that the local church in Bithynia sings 'a hymn to Christ as a god'. In short, as most early hymns demonstrate, it is the content, usually trinitarian and objectively doctrinal, that provides the essential heart of the hymns in corporate Christian worship in those early centuries. As the years went by, the tension between objective and subjective grew and remained a feature throughout Christian history.

What then are my goals in writing hymns ? First, to express truth as it is grounded in Holy Scripture and to do so in language which, while theological, carries contemporary force and lifts the heart and mind of the singing congregation to God, as it touches them at the deepest level of their personalities.

Standing as I do, an Anglican within the Evangelical tradition, I am doubly conscious of that tension and I welcome it. My very first hymn, written in 1952 (and long since lost), was clearly, and unwittingly, on the subjective side. By 1962, after six years of ordained ministry, I was consciously beginning to aim for a more objective content, though not ignoring the responsive element. That has remained my goal ever since. A good hymn should teach truth, and not merely leave the singer feeling warmed up.

xi

The construction, shape, and balance of my verse has deep roots. As a small boy, from A.A. Milne onwards, I have loved poetry and the English language. I owe a huge debt to two elderly spinster ladies who taught me in their 'dame' school not only to learn reams of it but to proclaim it publicly on Parents' Days and the like. Words, in consequence, came to occupy a potent place in my life and the sound and feel of them, sung or spoken, has been a lifelong pleasure and real discipline. The blend of metre, rhyme, and stress remains a constant element not only in what I write but also in my editorial tasks and in the adjudication of hymn competitions which have been a significant part of my ministry in the past twenty years.

As a chorister, choirman, and choirmaster (though long in the past), hymns acquired a major place in my writing and singing and thus took their place in my spiritual development and aesthetic enjoyment. As Jubilate Hymns have sought to express it, the coupling of 'quality texts to quality tunes' has been a regular feature of my goals. Personally, I have only ever attempted one tune ('Somerset', rudely described by my Jubilate colleagues as 'Michael's Somerset drinking song') which appeared in *Psalm Praise* to a metrical version of Psalm 111. It has only ever been mentioned subsequently in Christopher Idle's *Light upon the River* collection (no. 248).

Unlike some of my hymn-writing contemporaries, I have never felt the urge to produce indexes of biblical passages, theological themes, lists of recordings etc. They provide a most valuable resource in major hymn-books but while undoubtedly useful to a small handful of professionals, the space they occupy seems disproportionate in a personal collection so I have not attempted to include them.

Incidentally, producing such collections is quite an expensive project and I am most grateful to both the Pratt Green Trust and the Jubilate Trust for generous assistance. Since both are charitable bodies, this book cannot be a commercial operation which is why it is made available as a gift. I hope you enjoy using it and making its existence known. It can be obtained from me at 6, Discovery Walk, London. E1W 2JG for the price of postage and packing. (This is charged at £1 in the United Kingdom and US $3.60 at the Printed Paper airmail rate)

I cannot conclude without expressing my warmest appreciation by name to those who have played a major part in the development of my work in the field of hymnody. I trust that those not explicitly named will forgive me. They also are worthy of my thanks but lines have to be drawn somewhere.

My grateful thanks, then, (in alphabetical order) to John Barnard, Timothy Dudley-Smith, Bunty Grundy, Christopher Idle, David Iliff, Steve James, David Peacock, George H. Shorney, Noel Tredinnick, Norman Warren, Paul and Merrilyn Williams, and David Wilson.

Above all, and not least for his generous Foreword, to Michael Baughen, a friend since we first sang together in the Choir at Christ Church, Orpington, at the end of the 1940s, and who has worked tirelessly to produce and encourage hymns for yesterday's, today's, and tomorrow's church, my undying thanks and warmest affection.

There is, according to Randle Manwaring, poet and hymn-writer, and long-standing friend, a German proverb which sums it all up so well:

> 'Speak and you are my fellow man.
> Sing and you are my brother and sister'.

Amen to that.

Michael Saward

Most widely published Saward texts

First line
Christ triumphant (143 books)
Baptised in water (38 books)
Lord of the cross (23)
These are the facts (17)
The earth is yours (17)
Wind of God (15)
King of the universe(11)
O Trinity, O Trinity (9)
O sacrifice of Calvary (9)
All-creating heavenly Father (7)
* Lord, your church (7)
Sing glory to God (7)
Through all our days (7)
Welcome to another day (7)
Christmas for God's (7)
Clothed in kingly majesty (6)
Come all you good people (5)
Happy are those (5)
Protect me God (5)
This is the truth (5)

(* joint authorship with the late Hugh Sherlock)

Saward hymns have been published in the following countries:

Britain (167 books); USA (32); Australia (5); Canada (3); Malaysia (2); and in 1 book in each of the Philippines; South Korea; South Africa; Ireland; Japan; Singapore and Norway.

A total of 215 books to date.

The above figures are accurate to 1st June 2006.

'Christ Triumphant'
the title hymn of this collection

'Christ Triumphant', already in 143 books around the world, is far and away the best known of my hymns. It was written in Elmer Gardens when I was a curate in Edgware, Middlesex, for the 28th birthday of the church's Young People's Fellowship and was my fifth hymn. I still have the original, scrawled in pencil, with corrections and cartoon doodles on a piece of rough foolscap paper. It was first published in 1966 in *Youth Praise*.

It was initially sung to E.G. Monk's (1819-1900) 'Angel Voices' but soon acquired fame to Michael Baughen's (b.1930) 'Christ Triumphant', which is still widely used for the hymn. John Barnard (b. 1948) wrote 'Guiting Power' (named after a Cotswold village) for the hymn at the end of the 1970s and it has taken over as the most widely used tune, especially on radio and television. It has even been background music to a kitchen scene on the BBC soap opera *Eastenders* as well as being sung at Westminster Abbey in the Queen's presence on more than one occasion. A German translation, 'Christ regiert, kann alles wenden', was made in 2003 by Karl-Heinz Schonfeld.

It has been recorded by various choirs including those of Salisbury and Wells cathedrals. It was sung at Archbishop Donald Coggan's Memorial Service at Winchester Cathedral.

Ironically, it is rarely used in the USA as some feminists object to Christ's self-description as 'Son of Man' and others reject the 'royal language' of the 'kingdom of God.' Since the latter is one of the most foundational doctrines of the New Testament it is hard to see what is gained by omitting a hymn which combines virtually all the great themes and titles relating to the person and teaching of Jesus.

The coupling of the words with 'Guiting Power' was described in print by Lionel Dakers, late Director of The Royal School of Church Music, as 'surely one of the great hymns of our time....a fine text enriched by a magnificent tune'.

1. Christ triumphant

Christ triumphant, ever reigning,
Saviour, Master, King!
Lord of Heaven, our lives sustaining,
hear us as we sing.
Yours the glory and the crown,
the high renown,
the eternal name.

Word incarnate, truth revealing,
Son of Man on earth!
Power and majesty concealing
by your humble birth.
Yours the glory and the crown,
the high renown,
the eternal name.

Suffering servant, scorned, ill-treated,
victim crucified!
Death is through the cross defeated,
sinners justified.
Yours the glory and the crown,
the high renown,
the eternal name.

Priestly king, enthroned for ever
high in heaven above!
Sin and death and hell shall never
stifle hymns of love.
Yours the glory and the crown,
the high renown,
the eternal name.

So, our hearts and voices raising
through the ages long,
ceaselessly upon you gazing,
this shall be our song.
Yours the glory and the crown,
the high renown,
the eternal name.

April – May 1964

Tune: Guiting Power   by John Barnard

1

GUITING POWER

John Barnard

Descant

5. Our hearts and voi-ces rais-ing through the a - ges long,

Unison

up-on you gaz - - ing this shall be our song: Yours the

Org.

glo-ry and the crown, the high re-nown, the e-ter - nal name.

2. A babe was born

A babe was born on Christmas morn,
revealing heaven's glory,
as angel throngs sang joyful songs
of incarnation's story:
'Christ, Christ, the Lord of all,
you'll find him in a cattle stall.
Peace, peace, to earth has come
in David's town this morning.'

The shepherds, cowed, in terror bowed,
appalled at heaven's glory,
yet, in the dust, they came to trust
that incarnation story:
'Christ, Christ, the Lord of all....'

In Bethlehem, of Jesse's stem,
beholding heaven's glory,
the child they saw among the straw
he, incarnation's story:
'Christ, Christ, the Lord of all....'

Now growing bold, their news they told,
describing heaven's glory,
for all around, amazed, they found,
at incarnation's story:
'Christ, Christ, the Lord of all....'

So now we sing of David's king,
ascribing heaven's glory,
and praise the name of him who came
as incarnation's story:
'Christ, Christ, the Lord of all....'

5 November 2002

Tune: Greensleeves   Traditional English

Written at Discovery Walk, Wapping, London, at the prompting of
Mark Birchall, following a carol which he had written shortly before his death.

3

3. All-creating heavenly giver

All-creating heavenly giver,
bringing light and life to birth
all-sustaining heavenly Father
of the families of earth:
We, your children, lift our voices
singing gladly of your love:
never-ending are the praises
rising to your throne above.

Ever-living Lord and Saviour,
breaking chains of sin and shame;
ever-loving intercessor
prayers are answered in your name:
We, your servants, liberated
at a fearsome ransom-price,
in your kingdom are united
by that mighty sacrifice.

Lie-conceiving wind of heaven,
breathing gifts upon us all;
life-enhancing Spirit, given
to enrich us, great and small:
We, whose talents widely differ,
now restore to you your own,
and in true thanksgiving offer
all we are before the throne.

Father, Son, and Holy Spirit,
blessing all within your hand:
full the cup that we inherit,
firm the ground on which we stand:
We, your people, undeserving
of the grace you freely give,
now and ever, in thanksgiving
to your praise and glory live.

1 November 1979

4

Tune: Mead House by Cyril V. Taylor

Written at Ealing Vicarage, London, for a Stewardship Programme
in the parish. An alteration was made in 1998 (verse 2 line 4) to
meet the need for inclusive language.

4. All hail, majestic Trinity

All hail, majestic Trinity !
All hail, eternal Unity !
O God the Father, God the Son,
and God the Spirit, ever One.

One living God, our hearts adore,
Three Persons, now and evermore;
and in your loving mercy kind,
salvation's promised hope we find.

O Trinity, O Unity,
our God, both now and ever be,
and with the songs that angels sing
we shall rejoice, all-glorious King.

11 June 2002

Tune: Church Triumphant   by J.W. Elliott

This revision was prepared at Discovery Walk, Wapping, London,
based on John Chambers' (1805-93) version of the Anglo-Saxon
hymn 'Ave, colenda Trinitas.'

5. Baptised in water

Baptised in water,
sealed by the Spirit,
cleansed by the blood of Christ our King;
heirs of salvation,
trusting his promise –
faithfully now God's praise we sing.

Baptised in water,
sealed by the Spirit,
dead in the tomb with Christ our King;
one with his rising,
freed and forgiven
thankfully now God's praise we sing.

Baptised in water,
sealed by the Spirit,
marked with the sign of Christ our King;
born of one Father
we are his children –
joyfully now God's praise we sing.

29 May 1981

Tune: Schonster Herr Jesu   (a Silesian folk song).

Many hymnbooks, especially in the USA, have set these words to the tune 'Bunessan'. The natural stresses of the text do not work well with this coupling. The words were explicitly written for the Silesian tune and the author regards the 'Bunessan' linkage as a disaster ! He gave short shrift to one American editor who asked him to 'improve his unsuitable mis-match' since it 'didn't fit the 'Bunessan' stresses' !

Written at Ealing Vicarage in West London, the second of three baptismal hymns produced in four days, for inclusion in *Hymns for Today's Church*. The hymn has so far appeared in thirty-six books, worldwide, and is due for a Japanese translation in the near future.

6

6. Beyond the grasp of human brain

Beyond the grasp of human brain,
great God, majestic ruler;
we may by faith, your presence find
in Christ, our risen master.
And all the power which we can use
through turbine, jet and motor,
is nothing to the power of Christ
who frees us from disaster.

For we believe, despite the power
of greed and lust and Satan;
which dominates the human will,
that sin can be forgiven.
In humble trust and confidence
no power our souls can frighten,
we spread your liberating truth
that speaks of love in heaven.

Yet, here, within your universe,
we struggle with the tempter;
he has no right to trick and trap,
no right to make us cower.
So, Spirit of the living Christ,
the saviour and the victor,
that we may daily overcome
uphold us with your power.

January 1968

Tune: Youth Praise 2 (no: 181)
by Michael Baughen and David Wilson

Written at Ellesmere Avenue, Beckenham, Kent, in readiness for the
Youth Praise 2 book. Two minor alterations were made in 1998 to
meet the need for inclusive language.

7. Christmas for God's holy people

Christmas for God's holy people
is a time of joy and peace:
so all Christian men and women,
hymns and carols let us raise
to our God
come to earth,
Son of Man by human birth.

Child of Mary, virgin mother,
peasant baby, yet our king,
cradled there among the oxen:
joyful carols now we sing
to our God...

Angel armies sang in chorus
at our Christ's nativity:
He who came to share our nature:
so we sing with gaiety
to our God...

Shepherds hurried to the manger,
saw the babe of Bethlehem,
glorified the God of heaven:
so we join to sing with them
to our God...

Infant lowly, born in squalor,
prophet, king, and great high priest,
Word of God to us descending:
still we sing, both great and least,
to our God...

1966

Tune: Every star shall sing by Sydney Carter

8

This carol was written in Shaw Street, Liverpool, but no specific
date was recorded. It first appeared in *Youth Praise 2* in 1969 and
was twice amended, in 1981 and 1998.

8. Clothed in kingly majesty

Clothed in kingly majesty,
robed in regal power,
God is over all

Lord of all, unshakeable,
throned beyond all time,
God is over all.

Greater than the river's roar
and the surging sea,
God is over all.

Changeless as his law's decrees
Crowned our holy King,
God is over all.

24 December 1971

Tune: Psalm Praise 110   by Norman Warren

This text is a paraphrase of Psalm 93 written at Ellesmere Avenue, Beckenham, Kent, as part of a tour de force in the early evening of Christmas Eve. Following the radio broadcast of the Service of Nine Lessons and Carols from Kings College, Cambridge, I wrote eight psalm paraphrases between 4.30 p.m. and midnight. Six of these were published, this being the second most successful. Those published included versions of Psalms 13, 24, 93, 99, 119, and 126.

That evening was the most prolific in my hymn-writing career! The six psalms appeared in a total of 33 books over a period of 31 years.

9. *Come all you good people*

Come all you good people and burst into song!
Be joyful and happy, your praises prolong;
remember the birthday of Jesus our king.
who brings us salvation: his glory we sing.

His mother, a virgin so gentle and pure,
was told of God's promise, unchanging and sure,
foretelling the birthday of Jesus our king,
who brings us salvation: his glory we sing.

To Bethlehem hurried the shepherds amazed,
with stories of angels and heavens that blazed,
proclaiming the birthday of Jesus our king,
who brings us salvation: his glory we sing.

So come let us honour the babe in the hay
and give him our homage and worship today,
recalling the birthday of Jesus our king,
who brings us salvation: his glory we sing.

December 1973

Tune: Gallery Carol   Traditional English

Written in St Matthew's Vicarage, Clancarty Road, Fulham, London, this has its roots in two lines from the old Gallery Carol 'Rejoice and be merry.' It was written in order to bring it more specifically into line with the nativity story in the gospel. As with so many traditional carols, the original words distorted what the gospel had said. This version has its focus on Luke's account of what happened, both to Mary and the Bethlehem birth.

10. Forgotten for eternity

Forgotten for eternity
is that to be my destiny?
Your face no more to smile on me,
oppressed by every enemy,
my soul enduring agony?
Oh answer me, my God!
Oh answer me, my God!

Restore to me serenity,
and in your gracious charity,
lest I should die, give light to me,
frustrate my gloating adversary,
uplift my soul in ectasy,
and I'll rejoice, my God!
and I'll rejoice, my God!

24 December 1971

Tune: Psalm Praise 69   by David Wilson

See the note with no 8 above. This was written on the same occasion. It is a paraphrase of Psalm 13 and is probably best sung by a soloist. It has been recorded.

11. From Nazareth in Galilee

From Nazareth in Galilee
the holy family came
and in Judaea's Bethlehem,
to angel choirs' acclaim,
the infant Son of God was born
and Jesus is his name.
He is Lord of the country and the town,
 and the town,
Christ is Lord of the country and the town.

The child grew up a carpenter
and laboured long with wood,
until he answered heaven's call
and in the Jordan stood,
baptised by John, his fate to be
alone, misunderstood.
He is Lord…

He ministered to sick and poor
he challenged king and priest,
he taught the gospel to his friends,
the greatest and the least;
he spoke of joys and sorrows at
the coming heavenly feast.
He is Lord…

To tax-collector and to thief,
to husband and to wife,
to Pharisee, to prostitute,
to those embroiled in strife,
to farmer and to fishermen,
he spoke the word of life.
He is Lord…

At Christmastime we sing of him
whose task was just begun,
a baby destined for a cross,
incarnate, God's own Son,
who reigns in glory evermore
with our salvation won.
He is Lord…

13 October 1989

Tune: God rest ye merry   Traditional English

Written at Ealing Vicarage, London.

12

12. Glory to God

Glory to God in his holy place
sing glory to him in heaven.
Glory to God for his mighty acts
sing praise to the Unsurpassed.

Glory, the trumpet's fanfare sounds,
sing glory with lute and harp.
Glory, with tambourine and dance
sing glory with strings and flute.

Glory to God, the cymbals clash,
sing praise with resounding chimes.
Glory from all who breathe on earth
sing glory, sing praise to God.

Before May 1970

Tune: Psalm Praise no 148   by Norman Warren

Written in Ellesmere Avenue, Beckenham, Kent. A metrical version
of Psalm 150.

13. God, in whose image

God, in whose image we are made,
strengthened to face life unafraid,
we adore you, stand before you;
filled with delight at all you give
morning and night that we may live,
to your praises, our heart raises,
joyful praises, gladsome praises,
to your honour.

God, who in marriage has begun,
through male and female bound in one,
culmination of creation;
give to your children love and peace,
patience and trust that will not cease,
to your praises, our heart raises,
joyful praises, ceaseless praises,
for your mercy.

God, in whose family we are heirs,
give sons and daughters to be theirs,
bringing pleasure in good measure;
that in the home that is to be
all may find fruitful unity,
to your praises, our heart raises,
joyful praises, heartfelt praises,
as our duty.

So, Holy Trinity above,
we, who rejoice to feel your love,
knowing gladness, tinged with sadness;
then, as we face the gates of death,
drawing at last our final breath,
to your praises, our heart raises,
joyful praises, heaven's praises,
in your presence.

14 May 2000   14

Tune: Lasst uns Erfreuen   from Geistliche Gesangbuch, Koln.

Written in Amen Court, London, for the wedding of the Revd Gor-
don and Jessica Giles. He was St Paul's Cathedral's Succentor at the
time and included the hymn in his book *The Music of Praise*. The
hymn was first sung in the Cathedral.

14. God is king

God is king, the nations tremble;
he is throned, the earth is quaking;
Lord supreme, the people praise him
'Holy, holy, holy!'

God is king, he calls for justice;
he proclaims his righteous judgment;
Lord supreme, the people praise him.
'Holy, holy, holy!'

God is king, yet all may know him;
priests and prophets heard his precepts;
Lord supreme, the people praise him.
'Holy, holy, holy!'

God is king, yet he forgives us;
bears our sins in his own body;
Lord supreme, the people praise him.
Holy, holy, holy!'

24 December 1971

Tune: Psalm Praise no 113   by Michael Baughen

See the note with no 8 above. This was written on the same occasion. It
is a paraphrase of Psalm 99. One slight amendment was made in 1999
to meet the need for inclusive language in verse 3 line 1.

15. God of the garden

God of the garden, Eden's land,
where plants and trees brought rich delight;
where man and woman pleasure found,
fulfilled in all things, day and night.
Creator, Father, thanks we give
to you, the author of our joys,
and yet, despite these gifts, we grieve
for all that humankind destroys.

God of the garden place of pain,
Gethsemane of darkest power
where Jesus wept in anguish torn,
and evil forces showed their power.
Creator, Father, Lord sublime,
our Saviour Christ was crucified;
he bore our sins, our guilt, our shame,
and conquered death the day he died.

God of the garden by the tomb,
where Mary sobbed that Sunday morn,
and as she stood, bereaved and numb,
mistook the gardener in the dawn.
Creator, Father, give us faith
to recognise our living King,
to whom, the source of love and truth,
our lives, a sacrifice, we bring.

God of the garden yet-to-be,
fair Paradise of heavenly love;
where Christ, our all-in-all, shall say
'Come, taste the Tree of Life above'.
Creator, Father, in the calm,
where ours is not to question why,
we'll sing our everlasting hymn
before your garden-throne on high.

8th December 1997

16

Tune: Ye banks and braes   Traditional Scottish

Written in Amen Court in the City of London at the request of the
Worshipful Company of Gardeners, of which Livery Company I was
a member between 1997-2001 while Canon Treasurer of St Paul's Cathedral.

16. God of the world

God of the world serene,
God of the sea so green,
God of the sky's blue sheen,
God of creation.

God of the human line,
God of the bread and wine,
God of the great design,
your new creation.

Jesus, the virgin's son,
Jesus, the holy one,
Jesus, the battle done,
for our salvation.

Spirit of God above,
Spirit, the holy dove,
Spirit of peace and love,
breath of salvation.

Trinity, one in three,
triune divinity,
face we can never see,
Trinity holy.

Trinity, source of light,
Trinity, shining bright,
Trinity, our delight,
Trinity holy.

25 April 2001

Tune; Three in One.   Traditional Czech song
                            arr. by Norman Warren

17   Words written in Island House, Key Biscayne, Florida. USA, to a
      ancient tune from the *Sadska* collection being played on a CD in the
      shop in Prague Castle earlier in the year.

THREE IN ONE

Czech folk song
arr. Norman Warren

Music arrangement: © Norman Warren/Jubilate Hymns

18

17. God who created light

God who created light
from his commanding height,
his voice was heard.
Through sky and sea and earth,
labouring, came to birth,
sign of eternal worth,
life through God's word.

Christ who was born to save,
standing at Lazarus' grave,
his voice was heard.
He who had healed the lame
called to the dead by name,
and from the tomb there came
life through God's word.

Spirit, whose mighty power
surges through every hour,
his voice is heard.
Strong as the wind he blows,
swift as a torrent flows,
and to the church bestows
life through God's word.

5 January 1986

Tune: Moscow   by Felice de Giardini

Written at Ealing Vicarage, London. The hymn was originally four
verses and began 'He who created...' It initially appeared in *Hymns
for the People* in 1993 and was significantly altered before taking
the above (and definitive) form in *Sing Glory* in 1999.

18. God you have chosen

God you have chosen, called, prepared,
your servants for this hour;
pour out your Spirit on their lives
with wisdom, love and power.

Give to them knowledge, virtue, strength,
that, humble and assured,
they may embody Jesus' peace
and stand serene, matured.

May they the risen Christ obey
and fearlessly proclaim
forgiveness for the sins of all
who trust his saving name.

As they give thanks for bread and wine
and at the font preside;
so let your grace be known to all
who in that grace confide.

Lay your good hand upon them now,
ordain them at this feast;
the royal priesthood may they serve
of Christ, our great high priest.

12 September 1993

Tune: Billing   by Richard Terry

Written at Amen Court in the City of London for use at the first ordination of Women Priests (though also suitable for all Ordinations). It was first used as such at Canterbury Cathedral on 8 May 1994 and at other cathedrals, in the same year.

19. Happy are those

Happy are those who acknowledge their need,
theirs is the kingdom of heaven.
Happy are those who know sadness today,
for God shall uphold them for ever.
Laugh and rejoice!
Sing and be glad!
Yours is the kingdom of heaven. Amen.
Laugh and rejoice!
Sing and be glad!
You shall be with him for ever. Amen.

Happy are those who are gentle and kind,
happy are those who show mercy,
happy the hungry and thirsty of soul,
for God shall delight them for ever.
Laugh and rejoice.....

Happy are those who make peace in the world,
happy, though scorned and insulted.
Happy, because they are pure in their hearts,
for God shall reward them for ever.
Laugh and rejoice.....

7 September 1984

Tune: Here's to the maiden   Traditional English
                                              arr. Noel Tredinnick

Written at Ealing Vicarage in West London as an entry for the BBC
Songs of Praise hymn competition. It was a winner, for which I
received an inscribed handbell. I deliberately aimed to provide a
folksong treatment of the Beatitudes (one of the set subjects) to
the bucolic tune 'Here's to the maiden of bashful fifteen'. The traditional opening word from the *Authorised Version* of the Bible was
'Blessed' but the Greek is quite properly capable of the translation
'Happy' and most modern versions use that idea. The special service was broadcast from St James, Piccadilly and the presenter was
Sally Magnusson. Among the judges were Sydney Carter and Cyril
Taylor.

HERE'S TO THE MAIDEN

English folk song
arr. Noel Tredinnick

1. Happy are those who acknowledge their need, theirs is the kingdom of hea – ven. Hap-py are those who know sad-ness to day, for God shall up-hold them for ev – er. Laugh and re-joice! Sing and be glad! Yours is the king – dom of hea – ven. A – men. Laugh and re – joice! Sing and be glad! You shall be with him for ev – er. A -men.

22

20. Happy those with deepest needs

Happy those with deepest needs;
knowing God they find their peace
with longing that can never cease;
the kingdom is forever theirs.

Happy those with grieving hearts;
who have known the deepest loss
and find their comfort at the cross;
the kingdom is forever theirs.

Happy those with humble souls;
who, within the mirror, see
the danger of hypocrisy;
the kingdom is forever theirs.

Happy those with hungry lives;
longing deep within each day
the Lord's commandments to obey;
the kingdom is forever theirs.

Happy those who can forgive;
who, when others' sins are known,
can never overlook their own;
the kingdom is forever theirs.

Happy those whose hearts are pure;
they shall see the Father's face
and find in him a resting place;
the kingdom is forever theirs.

Happy those who seek for peace;
in the midst of toil and strife
God reveals eternal life;
the kingdom is forever theirs.

23   Happy those who pay the price;
persecution comes to those
who keep the faith despite God's foes
the kingdom is forever theirs.

(continued)

(continued)

These are truths that Jesus taught;
to disciples on the hill,
and to those who follow still;
'the kingdom is forever yours.'

18 April 2001

Tune: Rittersberk   Traditional Czech song
                             arr. by Norman Warren

See the note on No 16 above. This was written on the same occasion. It is a paraphrase of the Beatitudes from Matthew 5 but striking a very different note, both in text and tune, from No 19.

RITTERSBERK   **Czech folk song**
                                           arr. Norman Warren

Music arrangement: © Norman Warren/Jubilate Hymns

21. Have you not heard?

Have you not heard? Do you not know
that Christ has died for you?
That through his death he conquered death
to pay the ransom due.

What shall we say? How shall we live?
Since through his word revealed
he calls on us to die with him,
deep in his tomb concealed.

Is there no hope? Is there no joy?
Yes! Bursting from the grave,
baptised in him we rise to life
freed by his power to save.

One in his death, one in his life,
in baptism restored,
we trust his promise, know his power,
and serve our mighty Lord.

15 February 1979

Tune: Binchester   by William Croft

This was the first hymn that I wrote at Ealing Vicarage, West London, and also the first of my four baptismal hymns, all of which are
to be found in *Hymns for Today's Church*. At that stage it was very
hard to find any hymns on the subject of baptism other than those
which were specifically child-centred. Michael Perry and I set out to
write hymns (six in all) which were concerned with baptism itself.
Needless to say, we both believed firmly in the propriety of infant
baptism.

22. How happy those who daily live

How happy those who daily live
by God's sublime decrees;
his holy work is their delight
they trust his guarantees.

They blossom like a fruitful tree,
well-watered, evergreen,
as day and night they meditate
upon his word serene.

And so they prosper in their time,
ignoring worldly guile.
No cynic's sneer, no scoffer's scorn,
corrupts their honest smile.

They know that judgment comes at last
to lay the wicked low.
Like dusty chaff he blows away
his godlessness on show.

The Lord keeps watch upon his saints,
their righteousness he sees.
How happy those who daily live
by God's sublime decrees.

15 May 1998

Tune: St Stephen   by William Jones

This paraphrase of Psalm 1 was written at Amen Court in the City of
London (with two other Psalms, 8 and 15) for *Sing Glory,* but none
was accepted.

23. I thank you, Lord

I thank you, Lord, with all my heart
whenever good men gather;
your works are great, sublime and just,
to study them is pleasure.
Unchanging is your righteousness
imprinted on my memory;
your tenderness I know so well,
for ever, Lord, I'll thank you.

I thank you, Lord, with all my heart
whenever I remember,
the way you fed the wanderers
so hungry in the desert.
You proved your power before their eyes
your covenant you've honoured;
the promised land was theirs at last,
for ever, Lord, I'll thank you.

I thank you, Lord, with all my heart
whenever I am fearful;
for I recall your promises
dependable as always.
Your truth and righteousness are sure,
O holy Lord, Redeemer;
I'm lost in wonder as I learn,
for ever, Lord, I'll thank you.

1970

Tune: Somerset   by Michael Saward
                        arr. by James Seddon

27

I wrote 22 pieces in 1970-71 intended to appear in *Psalm Praise* (of which 19 were actually published in the book). All were written in Ellesmere Avenue, Beckenham, Kent. Foolishly, under much pressure, I did not record the exact date of seven of these. The above text is a paraphrase of Psalm 111. The tune (my only attempt) was whistled into a tape recorder while lying in the bath and handed to my friend Jim Seddon, who duly arranged it for publication.

SOMERSET

Michael Saward
arr. James Seddon

I thank You, Lord, with all my heart When ev - er good men ga - ther, Your

works are great, sub-lime and just, To stu - dy them is plea - sure. Un -

chang - ing is Your right-eous-ness Im-print - ed on my mem'- ry Your

ten - der-ness I know so well, For ev - er, Lord, I'll thank You.

24. I was glad

I was glad when I heard them say,
'we are going to God's own house',
and at last our feet are standing
at the gates of the City of Peace.

It's a city where all are one
in a union that's secure;
and all God's people are moving
to the gates of the City of Peace.

We are coming to praise his name
as he ordered his folk of old;
we'll stand at the place of justice
in the gates of the City of Peace.

We pray for the citizens' peace
and prosperity to you all,
who now are joyfully entering
through the gates of the City of Peace.

My friends and my brothers, I pray
that God's blessing be with you now;
for he's at the heart of all things
when we live in the City of Peace.

18 September 1971

Tune: Psalm Praise 131   by Norman Warren

This is a paraphrase of Psalm 122, written for *Psalm Praise*. Clearly
the original focus was on Jerusalem and its temple and Salem means
'peace.' Thus we pray for 'the City of Peace.' One of history's great
and tragic ironies is the reality that Jerusalem, the City of Peace and
justice, has all too often been a place of division and deep bitterness.
No wonder the Psalmist calls on everyone to pray for the city.

25. In awe and wonder

In awe and wonder, Lord our God,
we bow before your throne;
such holiness and burning love
are yours, and yours alone.

Angelic spirits, night and day,
adore your name on high.
eternal Lord in majesty
you hear their ceaseless cry.

'O holy, holy, holy Lord,
great God of power and might,
all-glorious in heaven and earth,
you reign in realms of light.'

Your holiness inspires our fear,
evokes, and heals, our shame;
your boundless wisdom, awesome power,
unchangeably the same.

Salvation comes from you alone
which we can never win;
your love revealed on Calvary
is cleansing for our sin.

There is no grace to match your grace,
no love to match your love,
no gentleness of human touch
like that of heaven above.

On earth we long for heaven's joy
where, bowed before your throne,
we know you, Father, Spirit, Son,
as God, and God alone.
19 October 1992

30

Tune: Westminster   by James Turle

Although a completely new hymn, this takes its origin from F.W.
Faber's 'My God, how wonderful thou art'. I wrote it at 1 a.m.
in Amen Court, in the City of London, on the day of the Jubilate
Hymns Annual Meeting.

26. Jesus Christ gives life

Jesus Christ gives life and gladness
to a world of death and grief;
love, to conquer human madness,
and, to broken hearts, relief;
hope for doubt and joy for sadness,
faith to silence unbelief.

Jesus in his incarnation
took our flesh, unique, alone;
on the cross won our salvation
nailed upon a wooden throne;
rising, laid the true foundation
of his church, a living stone.

Jesus works through us, expressing
to the nations in their need
his great love; that all possessing
faith and hope, from bondage freed,
round the globe may join, confessing
'Jesus Christ is life indeed'.

20 September 1982

Tune: Regent Square   by Henry T. Smart

In 1982 the Bible Churchmen's Missionary Society, (now renamed 'Crosslinks'), to celebrate its 60th anniversary took the theme 'Jesus Christ gives life'. I, having spent twelve years (1964-76) on the Society's General and Executive Committees, wrote this hymn specially for the occasion. Its two most recent appearances, in 1999 and 2000, have been limited to verses 1 and 3. It is in four hymnbooks.

27. King of the universe

King of the universe, Lord of the ages,
maker of all things, sustainer of life;
source of authority, wise and just creator,
hope of the nations: we praise and adore.

Powerful in majesty, throned in the heavens –
sun, moon and stars by your word are upheld;
time and eternity bow within your presence,
Lord of the nations: we praise and adore.

Wisdom unsearchable, fathomless knowledge
past understanding by our clever brain;
ground of reality, basis of all order,
guide to the nations: we praise and adore.

Justice and righteousness, holy, unswerving –
all that is tainted shall burn in your flame;
sword-bearing deity, punisher of evil,
judge of the nations: we praise and adore.

Ruler and potentate, sage and lawgiver,
humbled before you, unworthy we bow:
in our extremity, show us your forgiveness,
merciful Father: we praise and adore.

27 April 1970

Tune: Russian Anthem   by Alexis Lvov

In its original form this was written at Ellesmere Avenue, Beckenham, Kent, and first sung in the chapel of Dalton House, Bristol, on
19 June 1970. In that form it appeared in *Songs of Worship* (Scripture Union) in 1980. It was radically re-written in 1981 and then
slightly revised in 1999. I wrote it specifically for Lvov's majestic
Czarist National Anthem, a regal piece of music, entirely appro-
priate for such powerful words, deliberately blending justice and
mercy.

32

28. Let us gladly with one mind

Let us gladly with one mind
praise the Lord, for he is kind:
for his mercy shall endure,
ever faithful, ever sure.

He has made the realms of space,
all things have their ordered place:
for his mercy...

He created sky and sea,
field and mountain, flower and tree:
for his mercy...

Every creature, great and small –
God alone has made them all:
for his mercy...

Then he fashioned humankind,
crown of all that he designed:
for his mercy...

He has shaped our destiny –
heaven for all eternity:
for his mercy...

Glory then to God on high,
'Glory!' let creation cry:
for his mercy...

1981

Tune: Monkland   by John Wilkes

Milton's famous hymn is, today, undoubtedly archaic and I had no
compunction in going for a complete re-write in readiness for *Hymns
for Today's Church*. A quarter of a century later I am proud to have
produced this version which speaks to a contemporary generation
in imagery which leaves 'tressèd sun' and 'hornèd moon' looking
distinctly not so much poetic as turgid and faintly ridiculous.

33

30. Long ago to London's city

Long ago to London's city
came a servant of the Lord,
sent to lead a holy mission,
facing pagan flame and sword.
By the Saxon tribes surrounded,
he, to peasant and to king,
spoke of Christ, whose church was founded,
and its story now we sing.

On the hill, close by the Ludgate,
this bold Christian staked his claim.
Built a house for godly worship
and Mellitus was his name.
From this early congregation
as the centuries have flown
spreads the gospel of salvation
from a cradle to a throne.

Down the ages, pain and pleasure,
joy and sorrow, guilt and grief,
have befallen London's people,
blend of faith and unbelief.
Still the church proclaims its message
of a God who never tires,
for he seeks to help the needy
and fulfils their best desires.

Father, Son, and Holy Spirit,
ever faithful, ever true,
for our nation, church, and city,
hear the prayer we raise to you.

23 October 2003

Tune: Corvedale   by Maurice Bevan

Written at Discovery Walk, Wapping, London, to mark the 1400th anniversary of London diocese, founded in 604. This hymn was first sung in St Paul's Cathedral on 24 April 2004 to the tune 'Corvedale', written by Maurice Bevan, who had recently retired as one of the Cathedral's Vicars Choral. He originally wrote it to Faber's hymn 'There's a wideness in God's mercy.'

29. *Let us now, as one, rejoice*

Let us now, as one, rejoice
and give glory;
for the man of God's own choice,
sing his story.
Dunstan bore the marks of grace,
pure and lowly;
we today his steps re-trace,
life most holy.

In our land his voice is heard,
Christ proclaiming,
faithful to God's sacred word,
sinners shaming.
Both to monarch and to men
truth informing,
that both church and state again
need reforming.

Primate, bishop, abbot, priest,
gifted teacher;
and, to greatest as to least,
faithful preacher.
We today his life recall,
sing his story;
as to Christ we pledge our all,
and give glory.

5 March 1993

Tune: Redland   by Malcolm Archer

I was rung up by the Rector of St Dunstan's Church in Stepney
and invited to write a hymn suitable for use in churches all over
the world dedicated to St Dunstan. Being a Canon of St Paul's Cathedral, which has links with Stepney, and knowing Dunstan to
have been both Bishop of London and Archbishop of Canterbury,
it seemed only fair to accept the commission. I wrote the hymn in
Amen Court, in the City of London.

REDLAND

Malcòlm Archer

36

31. Lord, I delight to recall

Lord, I delight to recall your commandments
and the perfection of your moral law;
teach me, instruct me, and thus I'll retain them
deep in my heart to the end of my days.

Keep me from falsehood and covetous grasping,
save me from insults and scorn, which I dread;
strengthen my soul by fulfilling your promise,
and, in your justice, give life through your word.

Then, by experience, I'll know your salvation
and will be able to answer to those
who, by their sneers, seek to frighten my spirit,
since, through your law, I've discovered your love.

So I shall walk in the pathway of freedom
and before rulers will speak without fear;
I shall proclaim my delight in your precepts.
Oh, how I love to observe your commands.

Do not forget that I trust in your promise,
this is my comfort in sorrow and pain;
some may deride me but I will remember,
you do not change and your justice is sure,

Though I get angry at such disobedience,
yet I will sing, as an exile, of home;
I will recall to my mind, in the darkness,
your love for me and your life-giving law.

24 December 1971

Tune: Epiphany Hymn   by J.F. Thrupp

Written at Beckenham (see No 8 for details) as a paraphrase of
Psalm 119 verses 33-56. Two very minor alterations to inclusive
language were made in verses 5-6 in 1998.

32. Lord of glory, in our darkness

Lord of glory, in our darkness
shine upon us with your light
as, when walking to Damascus,
Saul beheld the vision bright;
filled with fear he learned your gospel,
then proclaimed it with delight.

He who served you in the Spirit
preached to Roman, Greek, and Jew,
and with burning love and passion
lived a message that was true;
Paul, apostle to the nations,
held the whole wide world in view.

Now, rejoicing at his memory,
in this consecrated place;
we recall the truths he taught us
and the hope of saving grace.
So, we worship you, Lord Jesus,
reigning King of time and space.

29 March 1993

Tune: Unser Herrscher   by Joachim Neander

Written at Amen Court in the City of London for, and first sung
at, the annual service of the Friends of St Paul's Cathedral, on 7
July 1993 at which I was the preacher in the presence of Queen
Elizabeth, the Queen Mother, herself for over 50 years the Patron of
the Friends. A couple of lines in verse 2 were re-written in 1998 to
improve the rhyme and it is the later version which is set out above
and duly published in two hymnbooks.

34. Lord, you've tested me

Lord, you've tested me and known me,
all of me is plain to you;
every purpose, every action,
seated, standing, lying down;
every thought my brain has fathomed,
every word my tongue pronounced,
you surround me every moment,
Lord, how wonderful you are.

Far beyond my meagre knowledge
is your character sublime,
can I flee your awesome presence,
or escape beyond your power ?
Heaven, grave, the farthest wavecrest;
In the darkness of the night ?
Still you find me, still you hold me,
Lord, how wonderful you are.

Every inch of flesh and sinew,
every blood cell, every bone,
from the hour of my conception,
planted in my mother's womb.
You have fashioned me and formed me,
shaped and spun me, watched me grow,
inexhaustible your knowledge,
Lord, how wonderful you are.

26 April 1970

Tune: Tor Hill   by Malcolm Archer

I wrote this while living at Ellesmere Avenue, Beckenham, Kent.
Taken from Psalm 139, I changed one word in 1999, altering 'puny'
to 'meagre' in verse 2 line 1. The former implies physical stature
whereas the latter rightly conveys a degree of inadequacy and better
fits the context.

TOR HILL

Malcolm Archer

33. Lord of the cross of shame

Lord of the cross of shame,
set my cold heart aflame
with love for you my Saviour and my Master;
who on that lonely day
bore all my sins away,
and saved me from the judgment and disaster.

Lord of the empty tomb,
born of a virgin's womb,
triumphant over death, its power defeated;
how gladly now I sing
your praise, my risen King,
and worship you, in heaven's splendour seated.

Lord of my life today,
teach me to live and pray
as one who knows the joy of sins forgiven;
so may I ever be,
now and eternally,
one with my fellow-citizens in heaven.

April 1963

Tune: Cross of Shame   by Michael Baughen

This, my fourth hymn, was written at Elmer Gardens in Edgware, North West London, for the birthday of the Youth Fellowship of St Margaret's Church, where I was Curate. It was first sung on 4 May to the tune 'Down Ampney'. It was later published in *Youth Praise 1* (1966) to Michael Baughen's specially composed 'Cross of Shame'. The final line originally ran 'united with the citizens...' but the stresses were not satisfactory and I altered it to the definitive version in 1981. I regard it as one of my favourite texts, not perhaps profound but touching the deepest levels of my faith.

35. My trust I place

My trust I place in God's good grace
his promises believing,
for now I see Christ died for me
my pardon thus achieving.

By water's sign this gift is mine,
my guilt has gone for ever;
for Christ the Son and I are one –
this bond no power can sever.

His word is true, my heart is new,
my life is joy unbounded,
for he will save me from the grave
while Satan stands confounded.

So now I sing of Christ my king,
his holy name confessing
who by this deed gives all I need
and fills me with his blessing.

30 May 1981

Tune: Dominus regit me   Traditional Irish melody

See Note attached to No 5 above. Written at Ealing Vicarage, West London, this is the third of my Baptismal hymns. Unusually, it appears in the *Dutch Reformed Hymnal* of South Africa which was published in 1990.

36. Now at last

Now at last,
your servant can depart in peace,
for your word
is finally fulfilled.

My own eyes
have witnessed your salvation, Lord,
which is seen
throughout the whole wide world.

Light for all,
revealing you in every land.
Glorious sight –
your people Israel's hope.

29 July 1987

Tune: Irstead   by Roger Mayor

This is a version of the *Nunc Dimittis*, the Song of Simeon in the
Temple in Jerusalem, (Luke 2 verse 29-32). When the infant Jesus
was 'presented', to fulfil the Jewish Law, these words were said by
a devout man as he held Jesus in his arms. These words have formed
part of the church's daily prayers since the 4th century. I wrote my
paraphrase in the lych-gate of Ealing Parish Church as I sheltered
from a thunderstorm.

37. Now sing my soul

Now sing my soul, 'How great the Lord!'
Rejoice, my spirit, in your God;
my Saviour who has looked on me
a humble servant in his sight.

For ever after, I'll be known
as happiest of the human race;
the mighty one has dealt with me
and holy, holy, is his name.

Throughout all ages, those who fear
his majesty, shall know his grace;
his powerful works disclose his might
he routs the arrogant in heart.

From thrones great rulers have been torn
yet humble men are raised on high;
the hungry have been satisfied
while rich men lack and creep away.

To Israel, servant of the Lord,
comes yet again the promised hope;
in Abraham and all his sons,
God's mercy ever shall endure.

Give glory then to God above!
Give praise to Christ his only Son!
Give thanks for all the Spirit's power,
Both now and through eternity.

22 May 1970

Tune: Church triumphant by J.W. Elliott

The *Magnificat* (from Luke 1 verses 46-55) has been used in the
church's liturgies since at least the 6ᵗʰ century. It records the words
of the Virgin Mary spoken to the mother of John the Baptist in response to the news of the conception of Jesus. I wrote this paraphrase in Ellesmere Avenue, Beckenham, Kent, in preparation for
Psalm Praise.

44

38. O Christ our God

O Christ our God, before your cross
unceasingly we bow.
You give us life, you give us hope.
The one eternal Now.

O Christ our God, before your tomb
we wait with baited breath.
The stone has gone, the clothes remain,
you've triumphed over death.

O Christ our God, most powerful Lord,
the true and living way.
You show the path to heaven above,
alive on that third day.

O Christ our God, the one true love,
your goodness all may see.
We gaze on you, enthroned on high
for all eternity.

3 June 2005

Tune: Contemplation   by F.A.G. Ouseley

In the 8th Century, John of Damascus wrote a hymn in Greek addressed to 'Christ the God' taking up the pagan Pliny the Younger's mention, in a letter to the Emperor Trajan, of early Christian worship which included a 'hymn to Christ as a god.' In the summer of 2005 I discovered a translation of the ancient hymn and wrote this new English version. It was first sung in Lichfield Cathedral.

39. O come, O come, Emmanuel
(See note at the foot of the text)

O come, true Wisdom from on high,
who orders all to mind and eye:
to us the path of knowledge show
and teach us in her ways to grow.
Rejoice, rejoice, Emmanuel
shall come to you, O Israel.

O come, strong Key of David, come
and open wide our heavenly home;
upon our journey give relief
and close the path to pain and grief.
Rejoice, rejoice.....

King of the Nations, come, embrace
and unify the human race;
command our sad divisions cease
and be for us the Prince of Peace.
Rejoice, rejoice.....

1999

Tune: Veni Emmanuel   Traditional French

The original Great Advent Antiphons numbered seven, but the great
majority of recent hymnbooks have, sadly, arbitrarily reduced the
number to five, thereby wrecking the intended pattern and order. Jubilate's *Sing Glory* is the only current book to have, first, returned to
the full sequence of seven and, secondly, provided a contemporary
version. I provided three of these stanzas (nos 2, 5, and 7) which
are set out above in that order. The full set of Jubilate words for the
Antiphons are to be found in *Sing Glory* as no 338.

40. O gracious God

O gracious God, we lift our voices high,
to praise your work in earth and sea and sky;
in music's tones, your triumphs we proclaim,
as we acknowledge your all-glorious name.

Eternal Jesus, crucified for all,
to your disciples, gone beyond recall;
to doubting eyes, you showed your power to save,
emerging free, the third day, from the grave.

Come, Holy Spirit, energize our search
that we may find your presence in the Church,
and, to the world, bring meaning from despair
as Christ's good news is taken everywhere.

Now, through your gospel-message, we belong;
we are your people and we sing your song.
So, we adore you, glorious Trinity,
and cry 'Amen', for all eternity.

17 August 2005

Tune: Anima Christi   by William Maher

This hymn was entered in a competition in the USA for a text on the
theme of the place of Music in Christian Worship. It was not given
an award. The words were written at Discovery Walk in Wapping,
East London.

41. O Holy Spirit, giver of life

O Holy Spirit, giver of life,
you bring our souls immortality;
yet in our hearts are struggle and strife,
we need your inward vitality.
Work out within us the Father's design,
give to us life, O Spirit divine.

O Holy Spirit, giver of light
to minds where all is obscurity;
exchange for blindness spiritual sight
that we may grow to maturity.
Work out within us the Father's design,
give to us light, O Spirit divine.

O Holy Spirit, giver of love
and joy and peace and fidelity;
the fruitfulness which comes from above,
that self-control and humility.
Work out within us the Father's design,
give to us love, O Spirit divine.

May 1962

Tune: Sussex Carol   Traditional English

Apart from the lost text that I wrote in 1952 as a theological student, (which in any case was never sung) this was my first hymn. Written at Elmer Gardens, Edgware, in North West London, it was deliberately set to a lively rhythm to counter what was then the very lethargic mood related to the work of the Holy Spirit. It was sung at the YPF birthday in May 1962.

42. O Sacrifice of Calvary

O Sacrifice of Calvary,
O Lamb whose sacred blood was shed,
O great High Priest on heaven's throne,
O Victor from the dead!
Here I recall your agony,
here see again your bloodstained brow;
beyond the sign of bread and wine
I know your presence now.

Your royal presence intercedes
eternally for me above,
and here my hungry spirit feeds
upon these gifts of love;
before your holy table laid
I kneel once more in hope and peace,
your blood and flesh my soul refresh
with joy that shall not cease.

1962

Tune: Sacrifice   by W.J. Walter

This, the second of my hymns, was written at Elmer Gardens in
Edgware, North West London, at some unspecified date in 1962. I
suspect I wrote it to be sung at a Twenty Club week-end houseparty
at Tonbridge in early November 1962 at the concluding service of
Holy Communion.

SACRIFICE

W.J. Walter
arr. David Iliff

43. O Trinity, O Trinity

O Trinity, O Trinity, the uncreated One;
O Unity, O Unity, of Father, Spirit, Son:
you are without beginning,
your life is never-ending;
and though our tongues are earthbound clay,
light them with flaming fire today.

O Majesty, O Majesty, the Father of our race;
O Mystery, O Mystery, we cannot see your face:
your justice is unswerving,
your love is overpowering,
and though our tongues...

O Virgin-born, O Virgin-born, of humankind the least;
O Victim torn, O Victim torn, both spotless lamb and priest:
you died and rose victorious,
you reign above all-glorious;
and though our tongues...

O Wind of God, O Wind of God, invigorate the dead;
O Fire of God, O Fire of God, your burning radiance spread:
your fruit our lives renewing,
your gifts, the church transforming;
and though our tongues...

O Trinity, O Trinity, the uncreated One;
O Unity, O Unity, of Father, Spirit, Son:
you are without beginning,
your life is never-ending,
and though our tongues...

June 1980

Tune: Trinity   by Kenneth Coates

51   Written on a rough scrap of paper in a tented camp at Cavalaire in
France, overlooking the Mediterranean, after reading Bishop Kallis-
tos Ware's book, *The Orthodox Way*. I based it on words from the
Lenten Triodon and I regard it as one of my most memorable hymns.
Kenneth Coates' tune, composed for it, fits the mood admirably.

44. Overflow with joy

Overflow with joy and gladness,
sing, my soul, for freedom gained;
God has wiped away our sadness
and the prisoners are unchained.
Gone the anguish, gone the sorrow,
gone the manacles of fear;
faith has triumphed, and tomorrow
shines with sunlight, bright and clear.

He whose hopes are in his Saviour,
he who trusts in Christ his Lord,
now proclaims by his behaviour
inward peace and true accord.
Like believers of past ages,
who for Jesus Christ were bold,
from such martyrs, saints and sages
no good thing does God withhold.

So, in gratitude, before you,
God our Father, sun and shield,
full of praises, we adore you,
as the powers of darkness yield.
For this mighty liberation,
after grief and torment long,
we rejoice in your salvation:
Hear, O God, our triumph song!

19 November 1991

Tune: Ode to Joy   by Ludwig van Beethoven

The editor of a national tabloid phoned to ask if I could write a hymn
to mark the release, that morning, from his 5-year captivity, of my
friend, Terry Waite. He needed the text within three hours! I faxed
the above with ten minutes to spare. The paper made a substantial
donation to Y-Care, the charity of which Terry was chairman. The
hymn was published in *New Start* (1999), the official *Churches Together Collection for the Millennium.*

45. Peace be with you all

'Peace be with you all', we sing;
peace from Christ, our lord and king,
he it is who makes us one,
God's eternal rising Son.

Bound together in his name,
welded by the Spirit's flame;
at his table here we kneel
and his living presence feel.

Bread is broken for our food;
wine we share in gratitude.
His the flesh and blood he gave
for the world he died to save.

So, with empty hands, we bow
welcoming our Saviour now
and, renewed in mind and heart,
in the peace of Christ depart.

28 August 1987

Tune: Song 13   by Orlando Gibbons

I wrote this hymn in Ealing Vicarage, West London, at the sugges-
tion on Tony Cruddas, who had been a member of our church prior
to his moving to Ashtead in Surrey. It is obviously meant to be used
in the latter part of Holy Communion.

47. Protect me God

Protect me God, I trust in you
I tell you now 'you are my Lord',
on you my happiness depends.
Protect me, God, trust in you.

Your people are a chosen race
and I delight in faithful friends,
but pagan ways I will not share.
Protect me, God, I trust in you.

Lord God, you are my food and drink,
my work for you is joy indeed;
glad is the heritage that's mine.
Protect me, God, I trust in you.

Thank you, my Lord, for warning me,
by night and day you guide my thoughts,
with you before me I stand firm.
Protect me, God, I trust in you.

So now I'm glad in heart and soul
for I have found security;
among the dead I shall not rot.
Protect me, God, I trust in you.

Not death, but life, shall be my path
abundant joy your presence grants;
an honoured place, and happiness.
Protect me, God, I trust in you.

Before May 1970

Tune: Bow Brickhill   by S.H. Nicholson

This is a metrical paraphrase from Psalm 16, written at Ellesmere
Avenue, Beckenham, Kent, in readiness for *Psalm Praise*.

54

46. Praise we offer

Praise we offer, Lord of glory,
for your coming to our earth;
called to be the child of Mary,
taking manhood by your birth:
praise we offer, Lord of glory
for your coming to our earth.

Praise we offer, Lord of glory,
for your passion and your death;
called to suffer for us sinners,
faithful till your final breath:
praise we offer, Lord of glory
for your passion and your death.

Praise we offer, Lord of glory,
for your conquest of the grave;
called to break the chains which bound us,
rising, faithful souls to save:
praise we offer, Lord of glory
for your conquest of the grave.

Praise we offer, Lord of glory,
for your Spirit's touch of power;
called to give our lives new radiance,
filling us from hour to hour:
praise we offer, Lord of glory
for your Spirit's touch of power.

Praise we offer, Lord of glory,
for the hope which all our days,
called to being by your labours,
turns our thoughts to endless praise:
praise we offer, Lord of glory –
endless songs of joyful praise!

55   23 January 1981

Tune: Gouldsbrook   by Malcolm Archer

This is a paraphrase based on a theme of N.F.S. Grundtvig, the
Danish theologian, poet, and educationist. It was written at Ealing
Vicarage, West London. Malcolm Archer is Director of Music at St
Paul's Cathedral, London.

GOULDSBROOK

Malcolm Archer

49. Rejoice, all creation

Rejoice, all creation, rejoice in God's love,
rejoice on earth and in heaven above.
Come answer his call to each and to all.
Rejoice, creation, rejoice in his love.

Give thanks to the Saviour, give thanks to his name,
give thanks to Jesus, from heaven he came,
transforming the earth with signs of new birth.
Give thanks, creation, give thanks to his name.

Sing praise for the Spirit, sing praise for his power,
sing praise to him who gives life every hour.
Our minds he renews his world to enthuse.
Sing praise, creation, sing praise for his power.

Bow down to the Father, bow down to the Son,
and to the Spirit, the three-ever-one.
This hymn we will raise throughout all our days.
Bow down, creation, to God, three-in-one.

13 July 2004

Tune: Klatovy   Traditional Bohemian folk song
                     arr. Norman Warren

See numbers 16 and 20 above for details. The words were written in
Island House, Key Biscayne, Florida.

KLATOVY

**Bohemian folk song
arr. John Barnard**

Music arrangement: © John Barnard / Jubilate Hymns

58

48. Redeemer, Lord

Redeemer, Lord, your praise we sing
and magnify your holy name;
your gift of oil to you we bring,
to us your saving power proclaim!

The sun in splendour warmed the ground
that nourishes the olive tree;
whose laden branches all around
give oil for our infirmity.

So now this oil be richly blessed
to us and all who feel its power,
and may your name, in faith confessed,
bring healing in a needful hour.

From those baptised, let Satan flee,
his evil malice be undone;
signed with the cross, the oil shall be
a symbol of the war begun.

In every service, every task,
may your anointing warm our soul,
that by your Spirit, as we ask,
the sign of oil shall make us whole.

Then let this time of vows renewed,
recall the Lord who died to save;
and at his table, heaven's food
proclaim his empty cross and grave.

17 April 1990

Tune: Herongate   Traditional English

The then Bishop of Willesden (Tom Butler) invited me to write a
hymn for the annual Maundy Thursday service in which the Clergy
renewed their ordination vows and shared in the blessing of various
oils at a eucharist. This was the result. The hymn has regularly been
used at St Paul's, and other Cathedrals.

50. Silently at Christmas

Silently at Christmas
Jesus came to town,
homelessness he suffered,
in a stable born.
Son of God almighty
heir to heaven's crown,
powerlessness he suffered
on that morn.

Hurriedly at Christmas
shepherds came to town,
guilelessness they offered,
in the humble barn.
To the Lord almighty
heir to heaven's crown,
lowliness they offered
on that morn.

Painfully at Christmas
people live in town,
hopelessness they suffer
hungry and alone.
Cursing the almighty
heir to heaven's crown
thoughtlessness they suffer
on this morn.

Willingly at Christmas,
Christians in our town,
joyfulness they offer,
carolling the Son,
and to Christ almighty
heir to heaven's crown,
selflessness they offer
on this morn.

Longingly each Christmas
Jesus comes to town,
godlessness he suffers,
how his heart must burn!
He is love almighty
heir to heaven's crown,
loneliness he suffers
on this morn.

60

12 October 1989

Tune: Cranham   by Gustav Holst

Written at Ealing Vicarage. West London.

51. Sing a hymn

Sing a hymn to God's great glory,
just and holy all his ways.
Let us tell redemption's story
singing songs of thankful praise.
God, who long ago created
music to inspire the heart,
lifts our souls, that stimulated,
we may play our joyful part.

Sing a hymn of Christ's salvation,
our Messiah, Servant, Priest;
building us a true foundation,
giving us a holy feast.
He who lived and died for others
from his virgin mother's womb,
now unites us, sisters, brothers,
through his conquest of the tomb.

Sing a hymn, in which shall feature
all the Spirit's living power;
animating every creature
day by day and hour by hour.
Sing, oh sing, in rhythm's motion
joining music, words and beat;
till the tongue and mind's devotion
in exultant worship meet.

Sing forever, all creation,
to the Trinity above.
Let the church in every nation
join in bonds of holy love.
Music of the highest order,
instruments and voices blend,
overcoming all disorder:
Songs of praise shall never end!

17 August 2005

61

Tune: Austria   Croatian folk tune
                       Adapted by Franz Josef Haydn

This hymn was written in Discovery Walk, Wapping, in East London, and submitted to an American hymn competition. It awaits publication.

52. Sing glory to God

Sing glory to God the Father,
the king of the universe, changelessly the same.
Sing praise to the world's creator
and magnify his holy name.
He made all that is round us and all that is beyond,
his hands uphold the planets, to him they all respond.

Sing glory to God the Saviour,
the Lord of the galaxies, bearer of our shame.
Sing praise to the world's redeemer
and magnify his holy name.
He suffered grief and torment, for sin he paid the price,
he rose in glorious triumph, both priest and sacrifice.

Sing glory to God the Spirit,
the power of the elements, setting hearts aflame.
Sing praise to the world's life-giver
and magnify his glorious name.
His gifts to all are given, his fruit transforms our hearts,
his fellowship enriches, a grace which he imparts.

Sing glory, the whole creation!
Give thanks to the Trinity, heaven's love proclaim.
Sing praise to our God, almighty,
and magnify his holy name.

25 June 1998

Tune: Prelude to the Te Deum   by Marc-Antoine
                                   Charpentier

For many years I had wanted to write a hymn to this marvellous
music from the era of Louis XIV and the decision by the Editors of
Jubilate Hymns to publish *Sing Glory* gave me the excuse to write a
theme hymn for the new book. It was given its world premiere at the
Royal Albert Hall in the presence of Margaret Thatcher, the Prime
Minister. My friend and colleague, Christopher Idle, thinks that it's
the finest hymn that I have written. It is currently in 7 hymnbooks.

53. Sing to God

Sing to God, whose loving mercy
hears the cry of those in need
and through purposeful compassion
heals the wounds of those who bleed.
We recall the battered traveller
by the road to Jericho,
who was saved by tender caring
on that journey long ago.

Sing to God, whose loving mercy
met a woman wracked with guilt;
one whose life was soiled and sullied
yet, whose richest perfume, spilt
on the feet of Christ the healer,
showed him not a heart of stone.
We recall his tender caring
as she sobbed, forlorn, alone.

Sing to God, whose loving mercy
faced the thousands, hungry, tired:
touched a youthful heart, providing
bread and fish, as was required.
We recall Christ's tender caring
and his followers, who obeyed;
they, in faith, saw baskets bulging,
and God's powerful grace displayed.

These, and many others like them,
face the anguish and the pain
of a lifetime's hard injustice
and humanity's disdain.
Glory, then, to God, whose servants
share the gospel Christ decreed,
and, like them, with full compassion,
joyful, sing to God indeed.

63

14 July 2001

Tune: Hyfrydol   by R.H. Pritchard

Written in Discovery Walk, Wapping, East London, for an American hymn competition. It has, so far, not been published.

54. Spirit of God, creation's power

Spirit of God, creation's power,
transforming shapeless space;
dynamic from the primal hour,
you poured out love and grace.

Spirit of God, at work in all,
refreshing history.
You motivate both great and small
with skill and artistry.

Spirit of God, prophetic source,
unveiling heaven's truth
through Christ, whose patient moral force
amazed both age and youth.

Spirit of God, at Pentecost,
surprising Greek and Jew
with tongues of flame you sought the lost
the whole wide world in view.

Spirit of God, your people's light,
awakening our search;
point us to Christ, our great delight,
revitalize your church.

So we rejoice, God's holy dove,
foreseeing Paradise;
and now await, moved by your love,
that final great surprise!

18 August 2001

Tune: Billing   by Richard Terry

This hymn was produced for the Christ Church, Louisville, USA,
hymn competition. It has, so far, not been published.   64

55. Thanks be to God

Thanks be to God
for his most holy Son:
Our hearts we lift
in adoration now.

Thanks be to God
for all the Spirit's power:
Our hearts we lift
in liberation now.

Thanks be to God
for giving us new birth:
Our hearts we lift
in consecration now.

Thanks be to God
for Eucharistic food:
Our hearts we lift
in exultation now.

Thanks be to God
for hope of heaven's joy:
Our hearts we lift
in expectation now.

Thanks be to God
blessed Trinity above:
Our hearts we lift
in veneration now.

30 May 1981

Tune: Song 46   by Orlando Gibbons

This brief hymn of thanksgiving was written at Ealing Vicarage,
West London, and published In *New Start* (1999), the official
Churches Together Collection for the Millennium.

56. The earth is yours

The earth is yours, O God,
you nourish it with rain;
the streams and rivers overflow,
the land bears seed again.

The soil is yours, O God,
the shoots are moist with dew;
and ripened by the burning sun
the corn grows straight and true.

The hills are yours, O God,
their grass is lush and green,
providing pastures for the flocks
which everywhere are seen.

The whole rich land is yours
for fodder or for plough;
and so, for rain, sun, soil and seed,
O God, we thank you now.

24 December 1971

Tune: St Thomas   from Williams's New
                                 Universal Psalmodist (1770)

A short paraphrase in metrical form of Psalm 65 vv 9-13, originally
for *Psalm Praise* and in 17 books. It is regarded as a harvest hymn. I
wrote it at Ellesmere Avenue, Beckenham, Kent, the first of the eight
on the night of Christmas Eve 1971. (see no. 8 for fuller details).

57. The kingdom of the living God

The kingdom of the living God
has come, as Christ proclaimed;
for he, the king, has, on his throne
the human heart reclaimed,
when, crowned with thorns, upon the cross,
his kingship has been named.

In action and in parable
that kingdom has been taught.
Its character, transforming lives,
is by disciples sought;
for Jesus, with the blood he shed,
has our salvation bought.

This king has our allegiance won,
our lives to him are bound,
he calls us as his royal priests
to treat as holy ground
the whole wide world for which he died
and rose, and now is crowned.

And yet we pray, 'Your kingdom come',
that holy city bright;
for he who came a peasant babe
shall come in radiant light
to bring that kingdom here on earth
and reign in glorious might.

24 July 1994

Tune: Kingdom   by Malcolm Archer

Written at Amen Court, City of London, for *New Start* (1999) the
official *Churches Together Collection for the Millennium* and later
included in *Sing to the Lord,* the St Paul's Cathedral supplementary
hymnbook.

KINGDOM

Malcolm Archer

68

58. The plan of God is sure

The plan of God is sure,
eternal in its scope.
it offers to the human race
its one enduring hope.

The truth of God breaks through,
revealing to the wise
his saving purposes, long hid
from unbelieving eyes.

The Son of God on earth,
child of the virgin's womb,
he lived and died, the perfect man,
resurgent from the tomb.

The church of God includes
the faithful of all lands;
both young and old, both rich and poor,
secure in God's good hands.

The reign of God is near,
peaceful and just its goal.
As Father, Son and Spirit rule
a universe made whole.

15 August 2004 (revised 25 November 2004)

Tune: Saigon   by Norman Warren

Written at Discovery Walk, Wapping, London, to be part of a Fest-
schrift for Professor John Montgomery's 75th birthday.

59. The Son of God

The Son of God rides out to war
the ancient foe to slay;
his blood-red banner streams afar,
who follows him today?
Who bears his cross? Who shares his grief?
Who walks his narrow way?
Who faces rampant unbelief?
Who follows him today?

The martyr Stephen's eagle eye
could pierce beyond the grave;
he saw his master in the sky
and called on him to save.
By zealots he was stoned to death
and, as he knelt to pray,
he blessed them with his final breath.
Who follows him today?

The valiant twelve, the chosen few,
on them the Spirit fell;
and faithful to the Lord they knew
they faced the hosts of hell.
They died beneath the brandished steel,
became the tyrant's prey,
yet did not flinch at their ordeal.
Who follows them today?

A noble army, young and old,
from every nation came;
some weak and frail, some strong and bold,
to win the martyr's fame.
Eternal joy to all is given
who trust you and obey:
O give us strength, great God of heaven,
to follow them today!

1981 (in this version)
Tune: Ellacombe   from Mainz Gesangbuch

Bishop Heber's hymn sounds very archaic today and very few contemporary books carry it. I thought it contained a range of splendidly powerful ideas and prepared this revision in readiness for *Hymns
for Today's Church* . It has since also been carried in *Praise*. I wrote
it in Ealing Vicarage, West London.

60. The Son of Man

This hymn is intended for pilgrimages to the Seven Churches of Asia (see the Book of Revelation, chapters 1-3). Each day the first two verses should be sung, followed by the relevant verse, and finally the last verse. This makes four verses each day.

The Son of Man has been revealed
as prophet, priest, and king
with feet like bronze, with robes of gold,
his voice a mighty torrent bold,
his eyes aflame, his age untold,
in glory shimmering.

To John he spoke on Patmos isle,
'Write now of what shall be;
don't be afraid, for there is none
before me, or when all is done,
I hold the keys, the stars, the sun;
stand up and you shall see'.

Ephesus
His are the words of one on high
who holds the stars in space;
who calls his faithful to endure
and, by repentance, to secure
the food of life, serene and pure,
within God's holy place.

Smyrna
His are the words of one on high
the first and last, who lives,
who offers hope instead of fear,
the crown of life to those who hear,
his glorious presence ever near,
as one who freely gives.

Pergamum
His are the words of one on high
who wields the two-edged sword;
he breaks the power of Satan's throne
he judges sin among his own,
and gives a name in secret known
to those who call him 'Lord'.

(continued)

(continued)

Thyatira

His are the words of one on high
whose eyes are flaming fire,
he flings the faithless to the dust
he pours his love upon the just,
the Morning Star is theirs, who trust
in Christ, their great desire.

Sardis

His are the words of one on high
who rules the seven stars,
and when he comes, as comes a thief,
all unexpected, bringing grief,
some will be lost in sham belief,
while white-robed saints bear scars.

Philadelphia

His are the words of one on high,
the holy one, and true,
who gives his church an open door,
and holds them safe in anguish sore,
who crowns the faithful who adore
his name, and city, new.

Laodicea

His are the words of one on high
all-glorious his renown;
he scorns complacency and pride,
for hungry sinners he'll provide,
he offers gold, refined and tried;
creation's Source and Crown.

To seven churches thus he spoke,
and called on each to hear.
Our fears and failures he'll expose,
our opportunities he knows,
his grace and mercy overflows,
his victory is near.

12 July 1997 and 7 March 2005

Tune: Revelation   by Noel Tredinnick

Verses 3-9 were written in Amen Court, City of London, the others
in Discovery Walk, Wapping, East London.

61. These are the facts

These are the facts as we have received them,
these are the truths that the Christian believes,
this is the basis of all of our preaching;
Christ died for sinners and rose from the tomb.

These are the facts as we have received them,
Christ has fulfilled what the scriptures foretold,
Adam's whole family in death had been sleeping,
Christ through his rising restores us to life.

These are the facts as we have received them,
we, with our saviour, have died on the cross;
now, having risen, our Jesus lives in us,
gives us his Spirit and makes us his home.

These are the facts as we have received them,
we shall be changed in the blink of an eye,
trumpets shall sound as we face life immortal,
this is the victory through Jesus our Lord.

These are the facts as we have received them,
these are the truths that the Christian believes,
this is the basis of all of our preaching,
Christ died for sinners and rose from the tomb.

6 June 1971

Tune: Yvonne   by Norman Warren

Written on Trinity Sunday at Ellesmere Avenue, Beckenham, Kent,
it has proved to be one of my most successful hymns. It was highly
regarded by Sir Norman Anderson, Chairman of the House of Laity
of General Synod and by John Stott, Rector emeritus of All Souls,
Langham Place. Some liberals have criticised my describing the
key ideas as 'facts' and 'truths' but that is, effectively, what St Paul
states in 1 Corinthians 15 on which the whole hymn is based. To
deny this is to undermine the very nature of the gospel which he
preached. I am unrepentant!

73

62. They who stand in awe of God

They who stand in awe of God are happy.
Hallelujah!
They whose joy is in his word are happy.
Hallelujah!
They are upright, they are just,
powerful heirs will follow them,
wealth and riches shall be theirs.
Sing glory! Hallelujah!

In the darkness they remain bright-shining.
Hallelujah!
Generous, merciful, and just, bright-shining.
Hallelujah!
Honest in their business life,
known for their integrity,
steadfast, they will be renowned.
Sing glory! Hallelujah!

Trouble cannot frighten them; they trust God.
Hallelujah!
They can conquer every fear; they trust God.
Hallelujah!
Freely to the poor they give,
theirs the justice that is sure,
honour is their true reward.
Sing glory! Hallelujah!

1 August 1992

Tune: Psalm Praise 120   by Norman Warren

This, in its original form ('He who stands...'), was written in about
1970 at Ellesmere Avenue, Beckenham, Kent, as a metrical paraphrase of Psalm 112. Two decades later, at Amen Court, in the City
of London, it was altered into a plural, inclusive-gender, form making it more suitable for contemporary congregational worship.

63. 'This do' the Master said

'This do' the Master said,
'this sacrament repeat,
my body and my blood
in holy symbol eat.
To this great feast I will invite,
and here unite, both great and least'.

Don't come, if you would boast
your knowledge and your might,
don't come if you refuse
to serve the Lord of light.
But those who sin has been confessed
may take their rest and join herein.

For you, whose sin he bore,
a promise he provides,
his covenant he makes
and at his board presides.
His sacrifice he'll not repeat,
but take and eat, and count the price.

One loaf, one body, we,
one family divine,
in sweet communion feed
upon that bread and wine.
The great high priest, until he come,
has now become our heavenly feast.

Then lift your church to heaven
where hunger is no more
and through eternity, O Christ,
we shall adore.
So make us share in glad embrace
your matchless grace, both here and there.

75   1962, amended 1968

Tune: Samuel   by Arthur Sullivan

Two of my first three hymns (this and no. 42) were written in Edgware. Hopefully, they demonstrate that a young Evangelical curate, writing for a youth group, even in the early 1960s, could regard a hymn for Holy Communion as entirely within the focus of such a group.

64. This is the truth

This is the truth which we proclaim,
God makes a promise firm and sure,
marked by this sign made in his name,
here for our sickness God's own cure.

This is the grave in which we lie
dead to a world of sin and shame,
raised with our Lord, to self we die
and live to praise God's holy name.

This is the sacrament of birth
sealed by a saviour's death for sin.
Trust in his mercy all on earth,
open your hearts and let him in.

This is the covenant of grace,
God, to the nations, shows his love;
people of every tribe and race
born, by his Spirit, from above.

This is the badge we proudly wear,
washed by our God, the Three-in-One,
welcomed, in fellowship we share,
hope of eternal life begun.

27 May 1981

Tune: Fulda   by William Gardiner

Written at Ealing Vicarage, West London, this is the second of my
four baptismal hymns (see nos. 5, 21, and 35 for the others). Three
were written within a period of three days. This was lightly revised
in 1999 to make it gender inclusive. It attempts to incorporate a
range of biblical themes identified with baptism.

65. Through all our days

Through all our days we'll sing the praise
of Christ, the resurrected;
who, though divine, did not decline
to be by men afflicted.
Pain, pain and suffering,
he knew its taste, he bore its sting;
peace, peace has come to earth
through Christ, our king and saviour.

His birth obscure, his family poor,
he owned no crown, no kingdom;
yet those who grieve in fear, believe
since he brought light and freedom.
Shame, shame and agony,
though guiltless he of felony;
shout, shout his sinless name,
our Jesus, king and saviour.

At fearful cost his life he lost
that death might be defeated;
the Man of Love, now risen above,
in majesty is seated.
Low, low was his descent,
to those by sin and sorrow bent;
life, life to all who trust
the Lord, our king and saviour.

And all who trust will find they must
obey the will of heaven;
for grief intense can make some sense
to those who are forgiven.
Hard, hard the road he trod
the Son of Man, the Son of God;
hope, hope in Christ alone,
our reigning king and saviour.

77

May 1967

Tune: Greensleeves   Traditional English

Written in Shaw Street, Liverpool, this was the winning entry for Southern TV's *Hymn for Britain*. It was lightly revised in 1981 and 1993.

67. Welcome to another day

Welcome to another day!
Night is blinded.
'Welcome', let creation say;
darkness ended.
Comes the sunshine after dew,
time for labour;
time to love my God anew
and my neighbour.

Welcome to the day of prayer
with God's people;
welcome is the joy we share
at his table.
Bread and wine from heaven fall;
come, receive it,
that the Christ may reign in all
who believe it.

Welcome is the peace that's given,
sure for ever;
welcome is the hope of heaven
when life's over.
As we work and as we pray,
trust God's story:
come then, as the dawning day
heralds glory!

September 1980

Tune: Gwalchmai   by Joseph Jones

Written at Ealing Vicarage, West London, for *Hymns for Today's Church*, I deliberately chose to use a dissonant rhyme pattern of the kind to be found in some of Wilfred Owen's poems. An example would be his unusual coupling of 'blade/blood/flash/flesh/leads/lads' in his *Arms and the Boy*. I was wryly amused when an ignorant secular journalist in the National Press complained that I couldn't recognise a rhyme!

66. We thank you, God almighty

We thank you, God almighty,
for our salvation won,
and for that faithful woman,
the mother of your Son.

For Mary's true obedience,
in answer to your call,
we thank you, God almighty,
her faith inspires us all.

We thank you, God almighty,
that, virgin at Christ's birth,
she was upheld by Joseph,
her husband her on earth.

And yet, through pain and sorrow,
her heart pierced by her loss,
we thank you, God almighty,
she stood beside the cross.

We thank you, God almighty,
despite her deepest grief,
she saw her risen saviour,
you honoured her belief.

And so, that virgin mother,
most favoured of our race,
awaits with us his coming,
when all shall see your face.

13 June 1998

Tune: Clonmel   Traditional Irish

This hymn, written for *Sing Glory*, is a deliberate attempt by an
Evangelical to provide a text honouring the Virgin Mary without
entering into the controversial territory inhabited by the Roman
Catholic doctrines which those in the Reformation tradition find
unacceptable.

CLONMEL   **Traditional Irish Melody**

68. When God delivered Israel

When God delivered Israel
from bondage long ago,
they thought that they were dreaming,
but soon they turned to laughing,
and sang the song of joy,
and sang the song of joy.

The godless nations round them
could not deny his power.
They cried 'O see this marvel',
'God's work' replied his people,
and so they sang for joy,
and so they sang for joy.

O God, restore our nation,
come, irrigate dry souls,
that those who sow in sadness
may reap their sheaves with gladness,
and sing the song of joy,
and sing the song of joy.

24 December 1971

Tune: Psalm Praise 134   by Norman Warren

This is yet another of the psalm paraphrases (126) which I wrote on Christmas Eve 1971 in Ellesmere Avenue, Beckenham, Kent. It has appeared in 4 books. I suspect that it is the first and only hymn or psalm text in which the word 'irrigate' has ever appeared! One of the modern Bibles translates the passage 'let us be like streams in the Southern desert'. It is referring to the Negev in Israel.

69. When things began to happen

When things began to happen,
before the birth of time,
the Word was with the Father
and shared his holy name.
Without him there was nothing –
all life derives from him;
his light shines in the darkness,
an unextinguished beam.

He came to his creation,
the work of his own hand;
he entered his own country
but they would not respond.
Yet some gave their allegiance
of life and heart and mind;
thus they became his subjects
and he became their friend.

Conceived by heaven's mercy,
this was no human birth;
for they are God's own children
redeemed from sin and death.
And they beheld his glory,
so full of grace and truth;
in Christ, God's Son, our saviour,
whom we adore by faith.

20 January 1975

Tune: Ellacombe   from the Mainz Gesangbuch

Written in St Matthew's Vicarage, Fulham, West London, this is
a straight paraphrase of St John's Gospel, chapter 1. As with no.
67, this uses the same assonant rhyming structure as is found in a
number of Wilfred Owen's poems. It is an interesting challenge to a
writer of verse and comes as a surprise to many people who are not
used to singing hymns of this kind.

70. Who can stand?

Who can stand on God's holy mount
or lodge within his tent?
None but the blameless and the pure
can make that high ascent.

Who can stand on God's holy mount
or lodge within his tent?
None but the one who speaks the truth
whose life is not mis-spent.

Who can stand on God's holy mount
or lodge within his tent?
None who has malice on his tongue,
no vicious malcontent.

Who can stand on God's holy mount
or lodge within his tent?
None but the one who keeps his oath
and saves the innocent.

Who can stand on God's holy mount
or lodge within his tent?
He who is noble, true, and good
finds God benevolent.

15 May 1998

Tune: Creator God   by Norman Warren

This metrical paraphrase of Psalm 15 was written in Amen Court,
City of London. It still awaits publication.

71. Who honours courage?

Who honours courage here,
who fights the devil?
Who boldly faces fear,
who conquers evil?
We're not afraid to fight!
we'll scorn the devil's spite;
Christ gives to us the right
to be his pilgrims.

Some may be terrified
by Satan's testing,
but faith is verified
when we're resisting.
There's no discouragement
shall cause us to relent
our firm declared intent
to be his pilgrims.

Though evil powers intend
to break our spirit;
we know we at the end
shall life inherit.
So, fantasies, away!
Why fear what others say?
We'll labour night and day
to be his pilgrims.

1981 after John Bunyan

Tune: Monks Gate   Traditional English
                        arr, R Vaughan Williams

In Part Two of *The Pilgrim's Progress*, Mr Valiant-for-Truth sings
'Who would true valour see?' In 1906 Percy Dearmer wrote a new
version, 'He who would valiant be', which rapidly overtook the
Bunyan words in later hymnbooks. The one major change intro-   84
duced by Dearmer was to introduce the holy 'Spirit' as distinct from
the human 'spirit' but he retained many of the archaisms. I have
further modernised the language (i.e. 'fantasies' for 'fancies' – the
same concept).

72. *Wind of God, dynamic Spirit*

Wind of God, dynamic Spirit,
breathe upon our hearts today;
that we may your power inherit
hear us, Spirit, as we pray.
Fill the vacuum that enslaves us,
emptiness of heart and soul:
and, through Jesus Christ who saves us,
give us life and make us whole.

Voice of God, prophetic Spirit,
speak to every heart today;
to encourage or prohibit,
urging action or delay.
Clear the vagueness which impedes us,
come, enlighten mind and soul;
and, through Jesus Christ who leads us,
teach the truth that makes us whole.

Fire of God, volcanic Spirit,
burn within our hearts today;
cleanse our sin; may we exhibit
holiness in every way.
Purge the squalidness that shames us,
soils the body, taints the soul;
and, through Jesus Christ who claims us,
purify us, make us whole.

May 1966

Tune: Treboeth   by Huw Williams

Written as a single verse in Shaw Street, Liverpool, for BBC's Radio 2 *People's Service* on Whit Sunday 1966 (originally sung, quite appropriately, to the tune 'Everton'), it was in 1968 augmented by two more verses and published in *Youth Praise 2* as 'Fire of God, titanic Spirit'. In 1998 some Jubilate colleagues strongly objected to 'titanic' for its pagan associations and the liner's sad demise. I returned to 'Wind of God' and changed 'titanic' to 'volcanic' which retained the 'fire' imagery from Acts 2. In 2000, Huw Williams, Sub Organist at St Paul's Cathedral, wrote 'Treboeth' specifically for the hymn.

TREBOETH

Huw Williams

86

Three jointly produced hymn texts

Please note that the copyright of these hymns varies from text to text and is set out beneath each hymn.

73. Come, let us worship

Come, let us worship the Christ of creation!
He set the numberless stars in their flight,
guiding the planets in accurate orbit.
King of the universe, rule us in might!

He is the image, the clear revelation;
in him there glows all the glory divine,
radiant in splendour, dispersing the shadows.
Light of the world, in our hearts ever shine!

He is our brother, the true incarnation;
unknown to many, disowned by his race.
He was forsaken, despised and rejected.
Suffering Servant, we share your disgrace.

He is our saviour, our hope of redemption;
he won our freedom, the victim who died;
spotless and perfect, his life-blood he yielded.
Lamb of atonement, dispel all our pride.

He is our victor, in whose resurrection
death is defeated, that we may receive
life for eternity, hope and forgiveness.
Lord of the grave, help us now to believe!

He is the giver, who since his ascension,
comes by his Spirit with gifts from above;
fills and renews us and gives us his kingdom.
Jesus, we long for the fruits of your love.

He is our monarch, enthroned in the heavens;
coming in triumph; yes, coming again.
Sin will be banished and we shall be with him.
Come, then, in majesty. Come, Lord, and reign!

4 February 1975   88

Tune: Epiphany   by Joseph Thrupp

© Frank Allred and Michael Saward / Jubilate Hymns
Frank wrote the original text (which needed a good deal of amendment) and Michael re-shaped it. We agreed that it should be 'joint-
authorship'. It is in four hymnbooks.

74. Let earth rejoice

Let earth rejoice! Let all creation sing!
Heav'n add its praises to the saviour-king.
Around the throne the shouts of triumph ring.
Alleluia! Alleluia!

To earth he came, a child so long ago;
light in our darkness, grace and truth to show.
The Word of life, whose gospel now we know.
Alleluia! Alleluia!

Despised, rejected, he was crucified;
suffering servant, on the cross he died;
true Lamb of God, salvation to provide.
Alleluia! Alleluia!

He rose again, and bursting from the grave
reigns high in glory, who our sins forgave;
now we rejoice, as those he came to save.
Alleluia! Alleluia!

So, on this day, O Christ, our mighty king,
let all the faithful, praise and honour bring;
our voices blend with heaven's choirs to sing.
Alleluia! Alleluia!

19 January 1995

Tune: Sine Nomine   by R. Vaughan Williams

© Peter Simpson and Michael Saward / Jubilate Hymns

Peter Simpson, a Roman Catholic priest, teaches at Latymer Upper
School in Chiswick. Michael preached for a school celebration at
St Paul's Cathedral where they met and in due course this hymn
was jointly authored.

75. Lord, your church on earth

Lord, your church on earth is seeking
power and wisdom from above.
Teach us all the art of speaking
with the accents of your love.
We will heed your great commission,
sending us to every place:
'Go, baptize, fulfil my mission,
serve with love and share my grace!'

You release us from our bondage,
lift the burdens caused by sin;
give new hope, new strength, and courage,
grant release from fears within.
Light for darkness, joy for sorrow,
love for hatred, peace for strife;
these and countless blessings follow
as the Spirit gives new life.

In the streets of every city
where the bruised and lonely live,
we will show the saviour's pity
and his longing to forgive.
In all lands and with all races
we will serve, and seek to bring
all the world to render praises
Christ, to you, redeemer king.

1960s (amended 1970s and 1999)

Tune: This hymn has been set to Lux Eoi, Everton, Abbot's Leigh,
Vision, and Ode to Joy. Take your pick!

© Hugh Sherlock and Michael Saward
(Methodist Publishing House and Jubilate Hymns).

Hugh's version ('Lord, thy church') was first published in 1969 in
Hymns and Songs and later in two other small books but its first
appearance in a major book was in 1982 in *Hymns for Today's
Church*. This was in my version. I had written to him in Jamaica
(where as a Methodist minister he was Secretary of the World
Methodist Council) asking whether he would approve of the
alterations and he replied agreeing to my proposal. Thus we accepted joint authorship of this version while he retained sole copyright of the original. He died in 1998.

Composers, arrangers(*), and sources

Archer, M	29, 34, 46, 57	Taylor, C	3
		Terry, R	18, 54
Barnard, J	1, 49*	Thrupp, J	31, 73
Baughen, M	6, 14, 33	Tredinnick, N	19*, 60
Beethoven, L van	44	Turle, J	25
Bevan, M	30	Vaughan Williams	71*, 74
Carter, S	7	Walter, W	42
Charpentier, M-A	52	Warren, N	8, 12, 24, 58, 61, 62, 68, 70, 16*, 20*, 48*
Coates, K	43		
Croft, W	21		
Elliott, J	4, 37		
Gardiner, W	64	Wilkes, J	28
Giardini, F	17	Williams, H	72
Gibbons, O	45, 55	Wilson, D	6*, 10
Haydn, J	51*		
Holst, G	50	*Traditional melodies as*	
Iliff, D	42*	*arranged:*	
Jones, J	67	Bohemian	49
Jones, W	22	Croatian	51
Lvov, A	27	Czech	16, 20
Maher, W	40	English	2, 9, 11, 19, 41, 48, 65, 71
Mayor, R	36		
Neander, J	32		
Nicholson, S	47	French	39
Ouseley, F	38	German	13, 59, 69
Pritchard, R	53	Irish	35, 66
Saward, M	23	Scottish	15
Seddon, J	23*	Silesian	5
Smart, H	26		
Sullivan, A	63		

I hope that you have enjoyed discovering this collection of my hymns.

You can find out more of the story of Jubilate Hymns by going to;
www.jubilate.co.uk

Sing glory the whole creation!
Give thanks to the Trinity,
heaven's love proclaim.
Sing praise to our God, almighty,
and magnify his holy name.